ABCs for Management Success

By

C.J. Hutchinson

ISBN: 1-4107-9907-7 (e-book)
ISBN: 1-4107-9906-9 (Paperback)

Library of Congress Control Number: 2003096725

This book is printed on acid free paper.

Printed in the United States of America
Bloomington, IN

1stBooks - rev. 09/22/03

Dedication

This book is dedicated to my daughter, Amanda,
who is just beginning her career.
May she always reach for the stars and succeed
in anything that she sets out to do.

Acknowledgments

I want to thank a good friend, Ashish Jain, for encouraging me to write this book. Without his constant urging for me to write it, as well as his steadfast belief that I had something to say that would benefit others trying to succeed in management, I would never have undertaken such a task.

I would also like to thank my husband Joe Hutchinson, my sister Wanda Steudl, and my brother Larry Mullins for all the drafts they read, suggestions they made, and encouragement they provided during the process of making the book a reality.

A special thank you to Pam Schutz, President and CEO of GE Wealth and Income Management, for reviewing my final draft, making helpful suggestions, and offering encouragement.

Table of Contents

Introduction

I have seen many frustrated managers unable to accomplish their goals because they did not understand how to get what they wanted, what it took to get there, or even where to start. Some of these same managers were their own worst enemy.

My purpose in writing this book is to cover some of the attitudes and behaviors you will need in order to help you be the success you want to be. These are all things I have learned over the years from my own struggles as well as from observing other successful, and unsuccessful, people. The topics covered in this book are meant to serve as an overview of the key things you will need to be aware of rather than a cookbook to go by. If you find something in these pages that is useful to you, something that you were unaware of, something that you need to improve on, or something that you need to start or stop doing, then I have succeeded in my purpose.

How do you define success?

Do you know yourself?

Do you know what you want out of your career?

Do you know what will make you happy?

Do you know what it will take for you to look forward to going to work every day?

Achieving Success

In whatever career you choose, achieving success is your ultimate goal.

It is a multi-step process made up of many small steps along the way.

It will take hard work and planning from you.

You must define what success means to you, what you want, and how long it will take you to achieve it.

You must know what it takes to get there so that you can create a plan of action.

You will need to stay focused on your plan to achieve the success you are looking for.

What kind of attitude do you have?

Does your attitude help you to be a success, or does it keep you from getting there?

Do you know that it will influence the way others act towards you and around you?

Do you know that it affects the way others perceive your abilities and your potential?

Attitudes for Success

Project a positive attitude. If this does not come naturally to you, then work on it.

Be an influence to others by having a positive, upbeat attitude.

Project self-confidence; let others know that you believe in what you are doing.

Believe in yourself if you want others to believe in you.

Speak with authority about the things you know, and others will be more likely to listen.

Show enthusiasm about whatever you are doing. Be a zealot for taking action.

Be optimistic; have a can-do attitude. The right attitude often counts for more than aptitude.

Be decisive. To be a leader, you have to be able to make decisions.

Be a good listener. You learn more from listening than you do from talking.

Treat everyone with respect. It should not matter who they are or what they do.

Have an opinion. Know why you feel the way that you do, and be ready to defend it with facts and data.

Be yourself, but work to be the best that you can be.

Do you make sure that the boss knows when one of your peers does something wrong?

Do you talk to people with the intention of finding out things that could reflect poorly on their work or abilities just so you can pass the information on to others?

Do you know that you are playing with fire, and if you play with fire, you could get burned?

Backstabber—A Potential Success Killer

Do not be a backstabber. You want to have more personal integrity than that.

Being a backstabber never pays in the long run. It will eventually come back to bite you.

The person you walk on to get ahead today could end up being your boss tomorrow.

If you do not get fired, your "new boss" will make your life miserable.

Get ahead on your own merits and accomplishments. Your success will be so much sweeter when you have earned it this way.

Who knows you better than you know yourself?

You know what you want.

You know who you are.

You know what you can do.

Believe That You Will Be a Success

Believe that you can be successful, and you will be successful.

Failure is no longer an option when you believe that you will be successful.

Believing that you can do something is half the battle for getting it done.

You know who you are and what you can do. Share that with those around you.

You may not think you are in sales, but you are selling yourself to others every day.

You need to market yourself, your abilities, and your interests.

Are you afraid of change?

Are you willing to take on new challenges?

Can you look at change as a positive thing?

Change Can Be a Good Thing

You need to embrace change, not avoid it.

Think of change as a positive thing, and it can be energizing.

Resisting change in what you do and how you do it is a career killer, not a career builder.

Change is inevitable in all companies at one time or another, so learn to use it to your benefit.

Those who embrace change and help make it happen are considered team players.

Be a change agent in your company, and there will be multiple opportunities for you.

Change agents are often given new challenges and responsibilities that help them attain success.

What is communication?

Is it important?

With whom do you communicate?

Do you cultivate professional friendships where you are now and maintain friendships from previous jobs?

Do you understand that we are talking about networking—and that it is very important that you start doing that now and continue doing it throughout your career?

Communication Is Critical

The most important thing in being successful is to communicate, communicate, and communicate.

Communication is the exchange of information between two or more people. Make sure the message you are sending is the message you intended to send.

You need to communicate in three directions: down to the people working *for* you, across to the people working *with* you (your peers), and up to your boss and others in management.

Each of these three directions is important to your success.

> The people that work for you need to know what you want in order to deliver it to you.

> The people that work with you need to know how and what you are doing to support you.

> The people that you work for need to know what you can do and are interested in doing.

Work on your verbal and written communication skills in all three of these directions.

Do you have open, honest communication with the people that work for you?

Do you talk with them or do you talk at them?

Is there a mutual level of trust and respect between you and those that work for you?

Communicate Down—With the People Working for You

Let the people working for you know *what* you expect of them if you want your expectations met. Talk with them until you are sure they understand what you want.

Let them know *when* you need something if you want to get the job done when you need it. Do not tell them something is needed tomorrow when you really do not need it for two weeks.

Let them know *why* you need something and how you are going to use it, so they will know the objective of what you are asking for.

Let them know *how* you want something to be done if you want it done a certain way.

Have open, honest communication with the people that work for you if you want them to believe you when you tell them something and trust your integrity as a manager.

Do you talk to your peers on a regular basis?

Do you talk to them about what is important to them and what they are involved in on a professional level as well as a personal level?

Communicate Across—With Your Peers

Communication about what you are doing allows your peers to understand your work and have an appreciation for what you do.

Communication with your peers provides a way to get to know them and what they do.

Regular communication will create a bond between you and your peers that will enable you to work together better as a team, instead of each person for themselves.

Regular communication with your peers will create a team player mentality that will make negotiations for roles, responsibilities, or resources easier when required.

Do you share your interests and plans with your boss and others in management?

Do you keep them informed about what you are doing?

Communicate Up—With Your Boss and Others

Communication with upper management includes more than your immediate boss.

Communication with others in management will allow them to get to know who you are and what you can do. If they know who you are and what you can do, they can see your value.

Communication with your boss and others in management about what you are doing will enable them to give you the recognition for your work that you are looking for.

If you think management should know what you are doing without you telling them, you could be right. However, it does not change the fact that you need to tell them!

Communication with management will give you the visibility you need to be seen as a key player in the organization—someone they do not want to lose.

Are you waiting for someone to hand you an opportunity?

Are you waiting for someone else to plan your career and tell you how you'll get there?

Control of Your Success Belongs to You

You control your career. Do not expect someone else to do it for you.

Be proactive in managing your own career if you want to be successful.

Make yourself and your abilities visible so that others will see your potential.

Be a self-starter and maintain the discipline required to complete your plan for success.

Your boss will usually work with you to help you be successful if you know what you want and have a plan to get there. They cannot help you if they do not know what you want.

Are you busy doing everything yourself while others around you have time to spare?

Do you think that no one can do the things you are doing as well as you will do them?

Is it your impression that you are supposed to do everything yourself?

Delegate When Possible

Effective managers use the power of delegation to accomplish more.

Most of the things that you think you need to do yourself can be delegated to someone else.

Learn to delegate responsibilities to others; it is good for you and good for them.

Do only those things that absolutely need to be done by you and delegate everything else.

When you do all the things that need done yourself, then you have no time left to manage!

Do you let commitments slide because they are small and don't seem that important?

Do you let commitments slide because they are larger than you thought they were, and you do not have time to do something that large?

Do you drop commitments because you were interested in them when you made the commitment, but then lost interest in them?

Delivery Is a Requirement

Delivery on commitments is not an option. It is very important that you do this.

Differentiate yourself by delivering quality work on time and on budget.

Always deliver no matter how small or large the commitment.

When you deliver on the smaller tasks, you will be trusted to deliver on larger tasks.

When you do not deliver, it is harder to get a second shot—not impossible, but harder.

Are you helping others achieve their goals?

Have you mentored anyone?

Are you worried that someone else's success will diminish your own?

Developing Those That Work for You Is Part of Your Job

While you are focused on getting where you want to go in your career, do not forget that the people working for you need your help to be successful.

They are depending on you for support, guidance, encouragement, and opportunities to achieve their own goals.

Be a mentor to those that work for you and see their abilities as an opportunity for you to help them develop their skills and interests.

See that they get the training they need to be able to achieve their goals.

Make sure that you provide the exposure they need so that they will be acknowledged for their work.

Never take credit for something someone working for you has done.

Always give credit to the individuals doing the actual work.

When those working for you succeed, it reflects on your management ability to develop others.

Would your friends and co-workers describe you as a slug or as a whirlwind?

If you were a light bulb, would you be a 10-watt or a 100-watt bulb?

Energy Needs to Be Positive

Have passion for what you do. It creates positive energy within and around you.

Share your passion with everyone that will listen; it may energize them.

Belief in you creates a positive energy that others will respond to.

Be energetic; know what you want and tirelessly go after it.

Use the force of positive energy to help you accomplish whatever you set out to do.

Are you thoughtful of your co-workers?

Are you a team player?

Are you ready and willing to help others when they need it?

Evaluate Your Behavior

Evaluate the behavior you display every day at work.

Are you concerned about others or only interested in yourself?

Do you go out of your way to help someone when asked or just brush him or her off?

Do you work for the good of the team, the company, or just yourself?

These are often the things of which you are judged.

Become aware of how the little, day-to-day things that you do are shaping your career.

Evaluate your actions and your reactions with people and situations at work on a daily basis.

People form positive or negative opinions of you from your everyday interactions with them.

Does fear of failure keep you from stepping outside of your comfort zone?

Are you willing to try new ideas and accept new challenges?

Do you know that fear not only paralyzes you but also paralyzes your career?

Fear Can Be Counter Productive

You have to be able to step outside of your comfort zone to achieve and maintain your success.

Fight the temptation to do what is easy because of your fear of failure if you try something new. Doing the same old thing over and over, the same old way, will not make you a success.

Do not let fear keep you from setting and achieving stretch goals throughout your career.

Do not be afraid to try an idea or something new and fail. You may fail many times before you are a success. The key is to keep trying until you get there.

Failure to try an idea or something new for fear of failing is counter productive to your success.

Do you complete what you start?

Does management have faith in you?

Do they know that you will complete whatever responsibility you have taken on, or do they constantly have to check on your progress?

Finish What You Start

Once you have taken on a responsibility, you need to follow it through to the end, regardless of the size or time commitment involved.

The job may be more than you bargained for. It could take more time than you realized and be more complicated than you originally thought when you accepted it.

Do not whine; no one wants to hear it. Finish the job to the best of your ability.

Be self-motivated to complete your responsibilities without needing constant supervision.

You want to be looked upon as someone that finishes a job even when it is not quick or easy.

You do not want to be seen as someone who starts something, creates a mess, then moves on to another job, leaving your mess for someone else to clean up and complete.

Your goal should be for management to know that once you have accepted responsibility for something, it will get done.

C.J. Hutchinson

What are goals?

Why should you have them?

What will they do for you?

Goals Will Get You There

You need to set and meet goals to be successful. Your goals should describe "what" not "how." They need to reflect what you will need to do to be successful in your job.

You need to understand the purpose of preparing goals. Your individual goals should support the business objectives, your department objectives, and your personal career objectives.

Goals will give direction to your work. They allow you to assess where you are and where you want to be. They also keep you in line with the company's strategy so that you are constantly moving forward without any missteps or wasted energy on the things that will not help you.

Success happens in stages. Decide what your objective is for each stage, how long you plan to take to get there, and how you will know when you have completed the goals that you set.

You first need to decide what your long-term goal is going to be. Your objectives should be clear to anyone that reads your goals. They should be concise steps that you plan to take.

Once you know your long-term goal, you can begin to map out a series of short-term goals that will help you to ultimately achieve your long-term goal.

Do you know what your goals are?

Do your goals and the company's overall strategy go together?

Goals—Long-term

Your definition of success is your long-term goal.

This goal should be in alignment with the company's overall strategy.

If your goal is at odds with the strategic direction of the company, then it will be impossible for you to meet your goal.

You need to realize what it will take to accomplish your long-term goal.

The "what it will take" part may be overwhelming at first glance.

Your long-term goal could and should take you years to achieve.

The secret is to have your long-term goal broken down into short-term goals that you can achieve in a reasonable amount of time.

Are your short-term goals doable?

Do you have a way to measure success for each set of goals?

Goals—Short-term

You need to plan for your success by setting multiple short-term, attainable goals.

By breaking down your long-term goals into short-term goals, you are creating a number of opportunities to feel successful along your career path.

Make sure that each set of short-term goals that you create is doable in a reasonable period of time. You need to set an actual date that you plan to achieve each goal.

Short-term goals should never be longer than one year in duration.

Have a way to measure success so that you will know when each goal is reached.

This method will keep you from getting discouraged before you have reached your long-term goal.

Do you share what you know with others?

Do you provide guidance or encouragement to anyone?

Help Others Along the Way

Always be willing to help others around you to learn, to grow, and to be successful.

Do not be afraid to share what you know with those around you or to admit what you do not know.

Knowledge is power and power is energy. Use that energy to help or be helped by others.

Remember that you may be an expert about some things, but you are not an expert about everything.

When you pool your knowledge to help each other, everyone benefits.

You need to learn from and work with others to be successful.

Do you know whom you should hire?

Do you know why you should hire them?

Are you willing to hire people that have skills and abilities that you do not have?

Hiring for Success

Someone who knows things, or has the ability to do things that you cannot do, is not a threat to your success.

You do not need to know or be able to do everything yourself.

Hire people that know and can do things that you cannot, and they will help you be successful.

This type of hiring will allow you to get more done, to do it better, and to do it faster.

It will provide you with someone to groom as your successor so that you can take on bigger, tougher jobs that will stretch your abilities and your value to the company.

Can you laugh at yourself when things aren't going the way you planned for them to go?

When you make a mistake, can you say, that was dumb, and move on to correct it?

Humor Is Your Friend

Do not take yourself too seriously; others will find you boring and avoid you.

Lighten up and enjoy your job and the people you work with.

The decision each day to be happy or miserable belongs to you.

Learn to see the humor in everyday events, and you'll enjoy your day more.

Do you use your imagination to think about things that are not possible today?

Do you still have dreams that you want to accomplish, or did you stop dreaming a long time ago?

Imagination Rediscovered

If you can imagine it, someone can do it.

Research and development depends on dreamers of things that are not yet possible.

When you were young, you used your imagination all the time.

You did not realize that the things you thought of were not possible.

As you got older, you were told your thoughts and dreams could not be done.

You believed that, so you gave up your dreams and ideas; you stopped using your imagination. That was a mistake. You need to get it back. It may take a while, but you can do it if you try.

Do not give up on your dreams and ideas. Just because something is not possible today, does not mean it will not be possible tomorrow.

Look for that new idea or new solution to an old problem, a gap that no one else has identified or found a solution for, or a new concept that fits the company strategy but has not been tried.

Free your mind of the "we have always done it this way" so that you can think outside the box. Be creative with your ideas and solutions. Let your imagination run wild.

Do you have personal integrity in what you do and how you deal with people and situations?

Does that integrity agree with the integrity of the company where you work?

Integrity on the Job

Integrity is not an option; it is a requirement.

It is important for you and important for the company.

The company is relying on your integrity because what you do reflects on them.

You are relying on the company's integrity because what they do reflects on you.

Make sure you can live with the choices and decisions you make on a daily basis.

If your gut tells you something is wrong with what you have been asked to do, then it is wrong for you, and you should not do it.

If it means you need to change jobs, then change jobs.

The cost of compromising your integrity will be too high a price for you to pay.

Success at the cost of your own self-respect should not be part of your idea of success.

Do you agree with everything your job requires you to do?

Do you know what to do when you do not agree?

Do you know where to draw the line between what you will do and what you will not do?

Just Get It Done

"Just get it done" responsibilities are requirements in every person's job.

You need to recognize the right of management to set the policies of the company and the requirements for each job.

You do not need to agree with everything required of you in your job, but you do need to acknowledge that it is something you are required to do.

You may not see the benefit in everything that is a part of your job, but that does not necessarily mean there is no benefit.

You cannot pick and choose what you will do and what you will let slide because you do not see the benefit of it and still expect to be successful at your job.

As long as you do not feel that something the company is asking you to do is an issue of integrity, then "just get it done."

If you decide to challenge company policy or procedures, pick your battles wisely.

Consider two things before doing battle: are you passionate about it, and can you win.

If you cannot support a company's policies and procedures, then you cannot be successful at that company.

Do you know your own strengths and weaknesses?

Does your ego keep you from getting help and advice from others when you need it?

Know Yourself

Know your strengths and your weaknesses.

Can you ask for advice or help when you need it?

You do not need to know how to do everything yourself.

You need to know how to get everything done.

Do only the things yourself that you are really good at doing.

Let someone else do the things that you are not as good at doing.

Do you have a big ego? Does it get in the way of your success?

Do not let your ego get in the way of being successful in your job.

Do you create communications or presentations geared to the audience that will receive them?

Can you tell when your message is not getting across to your audience?

Know Your Audience

The same communication style does not work with everyone.

Know the person or group you are communicating with and what works for them.

Some people respond to words and others need pictures.

Adjust your communications and presentations to your audience's needs.

Know how to read the body language of your audience when doing oral presentations.

Change your style of communicating in mid-stream, if necessary.

When is the last time you learned something new? Today...yesterday...last week?

Learning Never Stops

Learn from everyone around you.

Be a sponge when it comes to learning. Soak up all that you can.

You have as much to learn from others as they have to learn from you.

Seek out people that can teach you things that you do not know.

If you stop learning, you stop growing; so, constantly look for opportunities to learn.

If you know more than everyone else in your circle of friends, expand your circle.

Do you like your job?

Do you like your job but not what you are currently doing?

Like What You Are Doing

You need to like what you are doing overall to be successful.

Success will contain many small steps along the way.

As you progress through the steps needed to achieve your success, you will like some of those steps more than others.

For the ones you do not like as much, you will need to keep your mind on your ultimate goal.

Remaining positive will help you stay focused and help you like what you are doing.

Perceive each step as the one that is taking you closer to your goals. Realize that you will get there much faster if you mentally see each step as a good thing—as something that will ultimately help get you to where you want to be!

Do you think you can be a success all by yourself?

Do you think you will be a success as long as others do not let you down?

Management Is Not an Activity of One

The *First Key* to being successful in management is to realize that you will not get there on your own, without help from anyone else, and that if you fail to succeed, it is your fault.

Many people think they can be successful all by themselves. They think that they need no one's help.

They are only fooling themselves.

Many people think that they have failed because others have failed them. They didn't get a break or they weren't appreciated.

They are only fooling themselves.

The *Second Key* to success in management is to know the three management directions that are critical to your success. You will need to manage down, manage across, and manage up.

> *Manage Down—These are the people that work for you.*

> *Manage Across—These are your peers.*

> *Manage Up—This is your boss and others at that level.*

Do you know the people that work for you and what their goals are?

Do you know what motivates them?

Are you working with them to enable them to achieve their goals?

Manage Down—These Are the People That Work For You

Make sure they know they can depend on you to support them in what they do.

Have an open door policy where they can feel free to talk to you about anything.

Know what motivates them because different things motivate different people.

Challenge them to try new things, to learn, to grow, and to increase their value to the company.

Create an environment where they can feel safe to try things and fail.

Help them to set and achieve their goals. They will look to you for direction.

Provide them with opportunities for advancement and visibility with upper management.

Provide them positive feedback whenever an opportunity presents itself.

Always be truthful with them so that they know they can trust you.

As a manager, you will frequently know things that you cannot discuss. If you are asked about these things, be upfront and honest with them. Tell them you know but are not able to discuss it with them right now.

There is no cookie cutter approach to managing your people.

Each person will respond to situations, environments, and changes differently.

> Deal with people in a way that is appropriate for them.
> Get to know your people!
> Be the kind of boss that you would like to have.

Do you know anything about your peers?

What drives them?

What do they have passion about?

Do they know you?

Manage Across—These Are Your Peers

Your peers can help you, or they can stand in your way.

They are your support group for dealing with your day-to-day challenges.

Pay attention to the concerns of those that work with you. They need your support.

Be there for them if they need your support personally or professionally.

Learn what they do and take an interest in their work.

Make sure they know what you do; they can be your best cheerleaders.

Have a peer partner that you meet with regularly who you can discuss anything with.

Provide positive feedback to them whenever an opportunity presents itself.

Peers need to work together as a team for the good of all. Do your part.

Are you talking to your boss at least once a week?

Are you sharing with others what you are doing?

Does management know what your goals are and your plans to get there?

Manage Up—This Is Your Boss and Others

You need your boss's support to move forward in your career. Ask for it.

Pay attention to the things that concern your boss and others in upper management.

Make sure that you always let your boss know what you are doing.

Discuss everything with your boss first before going around them about something.

Never let your boss be blindsided by something that you should have told him or her.

Never make your boss look bad or correct them in front of anyone else.

Be willing to take on new challenges when your boss needs something done.

Deliver what you have been asked to do so your boss knows you can be counted on.

Ask for advice on your career planning. Your boss knows the ropes and will help you.

Do you find yourself complaining about something all the time?

Do the people that seek you out always want to complain to you about something or someone?

Do you know this is something you have to correct if you want to be successful?

Negativity Is Never Good for Success

Avoid being a negative person. If this does not come naturally, you need to work on it.

Negativity will become an anchor around your neck. It can take you under.

Stay away from people who are always negative; they will bring you down emotionally.

Avoid negative people; they will eventually make you negative as well.

Negative people will have a negative impact on you professionally.

When others have a negative impression about you, it can cause you to lose opportunities you would be interested in and qualified for.

Do you feel comfortable negotiating with others for the things you need or want?

Do you know what it takes to be successful in negotiations?

Negotiation Is Ongoing

Negotiation involves two or more people coming to an agreement either directly or with the assistance of a mediator or arbitrator.

Negotiation skills are critical to being successful.

Negotiations concerning your job are not over once you have been hired.

You will negotiate with people each and every day for what you need to get your job done.

You will need to negotiate with your staff from time to time for things that need to be done. This will be easier to do if you have been managing down.

You will need to negotiate with other teams for time or resources to get a job done. This will be easier to do if you have been managing across.

You will need to negotiate with your boss to get time, money, and resources to do your job. This will be easier if you have been managing up.

Successful negotiations will be a win for everyone involved.

Do you constantly second-guess your decisions?

What do you do when something does not work out the way you planned?

Never Look Back

Once you make a decision, never look back.

Do not waste energy second-guessing your decisions.

Use your energy to move forward to implement the decision you made.

If things do not work out the way you planned, then make a new plan.

Moving forward is the only direction you want to go.

Do others often disappoint you with the work they do?

Do you know how to get things done the way you want them done?

No One Is a Mind Reader

To prevent being disappointed by someone's work, you must:

> Explain exactly what you want.
> Explain what the information or end product should look like.
> Explain when and why you need it.
> Explain how you plan to use the information or product.
> Make sure your request is understood.

Where do you find opportunities?

Where do opportunities come from?

Why do others seem to get them and you do not?

Opportunity Is Everywhere

One of the most important things you must learn is to recognize an opportunity when it presents itself. Be alert at all times.

Opportunities are everywhere. You need to look for them wherever you go and in everything you do. Be relentless in your search.

You never know from where your next opportunity will come.

Any opportunity that is missed may not come around again.

Once you recognize an opportunity, do not be afraid to go after it.

If you do not see an opportunity, then try to create one.

C.J. Hutchinson

Do you wake up thinking you'll have a great day?

Do you dread the day ahead and wonder what surprises are in store for you to ruin the day?

Which of these two options will help you to be a success?

Optimistic Outlook Is Helpful

See your glass as half full instead of half empty.

Find the silver lining in any situation. It is there if you look.

Always take the high road. You will be glad you did.

Give people the benefit of the doubt. They may surprise you.

Deal with those around you in a pleasant and positive way.

Choose to have a good day instead of a bad one.

Do you know what you want?

Do you have any idea how long it will take you to get it?

Are you determined to get what you want no matter how long it takes?

Persistence Pays Off

One difference between those who are successful and those who are not successful is persistence.

Success does not just happen; you have to make it happen.

Know what you want and do not give up until you get it.

Do not let others talk you out of what you want. Make your own decisions.

Do not give up just because the going gets tough. You will make it if you stick with it.

You may have setbacks along the way; most people do, so expect them.

Remember that anything you really want is worth working for.

You *can* do it if you persevere. You *will* do it if you persevere.

Are you aware of what the politics are in your organization?

Do you know how to play the game if you need to?

Politics Exist in Every Company

Every office in every company has its version of politics.

Know what the politics are in your company.

Know who is political and who is not.

Know if reaching your goal depends on you being a political player.

If the answer is yes, then you need to learn how to play the game.

The only way to consistently accomplish what you set out to do, and have any influence in the organization, is to understand the politics of the organization.

Are you comfortable letting the quality of your work speak for who you are?

Do you know about Six Sigma Methodologies?

Are you trained on what Six Sigma is and how to use it?

Quality Comes in Two Forms

First is the Quality of the Work You Do.

Make sure that anything you do is done to the best of your ability.

The quality of your work says something about who you are.

Do not cut corners to save time or money at the cost of a quality product.

Do not do the easiest thing if it is not the best thing to do.

Quality needs to be a part of your personal work ethic no matter where you work.

Second is a Process Methodology.

Many companies use Six Sigma quality methodology.

This is all about process improvement. It is a statistical measurement of 3.4 defects per million. It is used to improve profits, cycle times, customer service, productivity, market share for your products, etc.

You define the process you are looking to improve and what your requirements are.

You measure the sigma level of the process as it is today.

You gather data to analyze the current state of your process.

You determine and then implement the improvement for the current process.

You then monitor the process to make sure it stays in control.

The tools and methods used in Six Sigma can be used to solve problems and make process improvements in any area.

If your company does not currently have a quality program, I suggest that you get a book on Six Sigma methodology and learn about what it is and how to use it.

Do you think people owe you respect because of who you are or what position you hold in the company?

Respect Is a Two-way Street

Show respect for others if you want to receive respect from them.

Every person should be treated the way you would want him or her to treat you.

Respect the people that work for you, those that work with you, and the people that you work for.

Respect their ideas, their opinions, their choices, and their goals.

C.J. Hutchinson

Are you good at scheduling your time?

Do you stick to your schedule or let others constantly interrupt you?

Schedule Your Time

Schedule your time and workload and stick to that schedule.

There will be exceptions to this rule, but they need to be exceptions, not an everyday occurrence.

Do not let others schedule your time with constant interruptions.

Just because they want help from you does not mean you need to put aside your schedule.

Explain that you have something that you need to do right now, but schedule a time to meet with them later.

An open door policy does not mean your time is their time at any and all times.

It means you are willing to talk to them about anything they wish to discuss.

When someone stops by your office unscheduled asking, "Do you have a minute?" politely say that you are busy, and schedule a time for them to come back and talk to you later.

Constant interruptions will keep you from getting your work done.

When you cannot get your work done, you are not scheduling properly.

If you are not good at scheduling, keep working on it. It is important to your success.

Can you work with others, or do you need to work alone?

Do you know how to be an effective team member?

Do you know how to create an effective team?

Teamwork Is Harder Than It Sounds

The importance of teamwork is often overlooked and under-rated.

Teams that work well together can accomplish much more than individuals.

Creating the right mix of team members with the right skill sets is important to the success of the team.

The team that works well together empowers each member to excel.

Teams where members work as individuals will be ineffective.

A dysfunctional team will take a project and the team under if not corrected.

It is critical to your success that you understand how to put a team together, how the dynamics of a team work, and how to manage the team and its individuals.

Are you prepared to accept new challenges?

Do you have the skills for new opportunities if they come your way?

Training for Your Success

Always continue to learn, grow, and challenge yourself to do new things.

The more you know how to do, the more you can do.

The more you can do, the more valuable you are to any company.

Make sure you will be ready when an opportunity comes. If you need additional training to get to the next step on your ladder of success, be willing to get it on your own. Do not wait for someone to hand it to you.

Getting one year's worth of experience out of fifteen years of work is of little value to anyone.

You do not want to find yourself out of work and discover that your skills are obsolete.

C.J. Hutchinson

Do you know what your job is?

Do you know why you were hired?

Do you understand that these are two different things?

Understand What Your Job Is

This sounds simple, but most people don't get it.

Is your job to advise upper management on how they should do certain things? After all, you have experience doing those things.

Is your job to advise upper management on what they should do in certain situations? After all, you have experience working on similar situations.

Is your job to advise upper management on what will and will not work in your area? After all, you have years of experience doing the things that work.

This is where frustration, anger, stress, and depression often set in.

You do not understand why they did not leverage your expertise before making a decision. They hired you for your expertise, but now they are not using it.

You could have told them that it was not a good idea. You have tried that before and know that it is a bad idea. They hired you for your knowledge, but now they are not using it.

You could have told them that it would not work. You have tried that before and know that it does not work. They hired you for your experience, but now they are not using it.

Are these things your job? No, they are not your job.

You are confusing what your job is with why you were hired.

You were hired for your expertise, knowledge, and experience.

Your job is to use those things to implement the decisions made by upper management.

The knowledge of what your job is will free you to do the job you were hired to do.

97

Do you bring value to the company?

Do you know what that value is?

Do you know how to increase it?

Value - That You Bring to the Company

Know what value you bring to the company and why it is of value.

Make sure that others know what value you bring to the company.

Always look for opportunities to increase that value:

> Volunteer for leadership roles or programs.
> Take an active role in community service.
> Learn new things and teach them to others.
> Look for exposure to upper management when possible.
> Build a functional expertise.
> Learn different areas of the business.
> Take a global assignment, if possible.

C.J. Hutchinson

Do you know the company strategic vision?

Do you know your role in accomplishing that vision?

Vision - Through the Eyes of the Company

There are two kinds of vision in any company. They are *strategic* and *tactical* vision. Both types of vision need to see the "Big Picture."

Strategic vision

Strategic vision is for the long-range direction of a company or department.

Strategists or upper management own this type of vision.

The "Big Picture" is critical for this group so they can identify and oversee all tactical changes that need to be made to achieve the strategic direction of the company.

Tactical vision

Tactical vision is for the long-range direction of departments or projects in support of the company's strategic direction.

Middle management or individual contributors own this type of vision.

The "Big Picture" is critical for this group so that they can identify and implement the tactical changes that will help achieve the overall strategic direction of the department.

Tactical changes usually involve process improvements in a function or department.

Every person, no matter what their job, can see tactical changes that would be good for their department. If it is good for their department, then it is good for the company.

What makes a person wise?

Where does one go to acquire wisdom?

Wisdom Comes from Everywhere

Wisdom can come:

> With age
> From training
> From experience
> From listening to and learning from others

Wisdom comes from all of the above, and the wise person knows that.

What should you expect along your journey to success?

e**X**pectations - For Your Path to Success

Expect to:

> Have disappointments along your journey.
> Suffer setbacks in achieving your goals.
> Be surprised by those you thought were friends, who were not.
> Be flexible on how and when you can achieve something.
> Change your long-term goals before your career is over.
> Work hard every step of the way to get what you want.

Expect to achieve what you set out to do. It will be easier to do once you expect to do it.

Do you know that you are creating your yesterdays today?

Are you using your time wisely?

Yesterday Is Gone

Yesterday is gone. Do not waste any energy on it; take care of today.

Do not keep looking back to say, "What if?"

Give one hundred percent to today, and all your yesterdays will be the best they could be.

How can you add the best value to the company?

How do you use that value to help you be successful?

Zero in On Your Ticket to Success

Zero in on where you can best serve the company.

Find something that does not work well and make it better. Think about what you are doing and why. Improve processes that you know could be better.

Find something that is broken and fix it. If a current process is broken, take the initiative to fix it.

Always look for non-value added work that can be eliminated.

Find a knowledge gap that would benefit the company. Learn it and teach it to others.

Whatever you do, be visible while you are doing it. Take advantage of the exposure to management when the opportunity presents itself.

C.J. Hutchinson

Conclusion

You need to know what success and being successful means to you. Know your career goals. Where do you see yourself in five years, in ten years? These are questions you will need to answer before you can create a plan that will turn your goals into a reality.

Once you decide what it is that you want, you need to know how to make it happen. How high do you want to go in the organization? The answer to that will determine the steps you will need to take to get you there. How quickly do you want to achieve your goals? The speed with which you want to get there will dictate how aggressive you need to be to make it happen.

Making it happen will take some of you longer than others. Hopefully, you have learned what obstacles face you, and you can start working on how to overcome them. If you need help, there are many books written on specific subjects that you can read, or you can select a mentor to work with—someone that you would like to emulate.

Whatever you choose to do, however far you need to go, I wish you well on your journey. I hope that you have been helped in some way by this book.

About the Author

C.J. Hutchinson was born in Lockwood, West Virginia and lived in Oak Hill, West Virginia until graduating from high school.

C.J. attended Lear Siegler Institute and graduated in 1970 with a degree in Computer Science. She worked for five years as a Senior Programmer Analyst in the banking industry in Washington, DC and Pittsburgh, Pennsylvania before leaving to spend six years as an independent consultant working for Rockwell International and Allegheny Ludlum International. She and her husband Joe have been married since 1972 and have one daughter, Amanda.

For eight years following the birth of her daughter, she owned and operated a children's thrift shop, keeping Amanda with her. Once Amanda started school, she sold the thrift shop and reentered the information management arena as a Senior Systems Analyst for Dollar Bank. After one year with Dollar Bank, her husband was transferred to Texas, where she spent four years as the CK4 Policy Administrative Director for Southwestern Life Insurance Co. The next three years were spent at Penn Corp Financial in Raleigh, North Carolina as a Project Manager.

In 1993, C.J. relocated to Orlando, Florida to join GE as the Manager of Administrative and Corporate Support Systems for Harvest Life Insurance Co. In 1998, when Harvest merged with Life of Virginia Insurance Co.—located in Richmond, Virginia—she accepted the position of Vice President of Life and Investment Systems. In 2003, she became the Data Reliability Leader for GE Wealth and Income Management.

www.ingramcontent.com/pod-product-compliance
Lightning Source LLC
Chambersburg PA
CBHW051441280526
45785CB00003B/1383